PETE PEPPER

Illustrations [illegible] *Reed*

PUBLISHED BY STUDIO PUBLICATIONS (IPSWICH) LIMITED
32 PRINCES STREET, IPSWICH, SUFFOLK, ENGLAND

Pete Pepper is one of the Munch Bunch.

He lives in a large flower-pot next door to his friend Tom Tomato.

Tom Tomato also lives in a flower-pot.

Pete Pepper is normally a very angry pepper.

One morning he was woken up very early by the sound of loud banging coming from next door.

Pete was very angry at being woken up so early.

Bang, Bang, Bang, he could hear.

"What on earth is all that noise?" Pete muttered to himself.

He got up and stormed into Tom Tomato's house.

"What are you doing?" Pete yelled above the noise of the bangs and crashes.

"I'm trying to knock this nail into the wall so that I can hang my painting," Tom replied.

Just then, as Tom turned round, he dropped his hammer right onto Pete's toe!

"Ouch!" cried Pete, turning even redder with anger.

“Oh! I am sorry, Pete,” said Tom, trying not to laugh.

“We are all decorating our houses today. Don’t you remember?”

“Well I’m not!” said Pete, and stormed off home.

He was a very cross Pepper!

Poor Pete Pepper!

First he was woken up early and then a hammer was dropped on his toe. He could tell it wasn't going to be a good day.

Pete looked round his room. Did it need decorating?

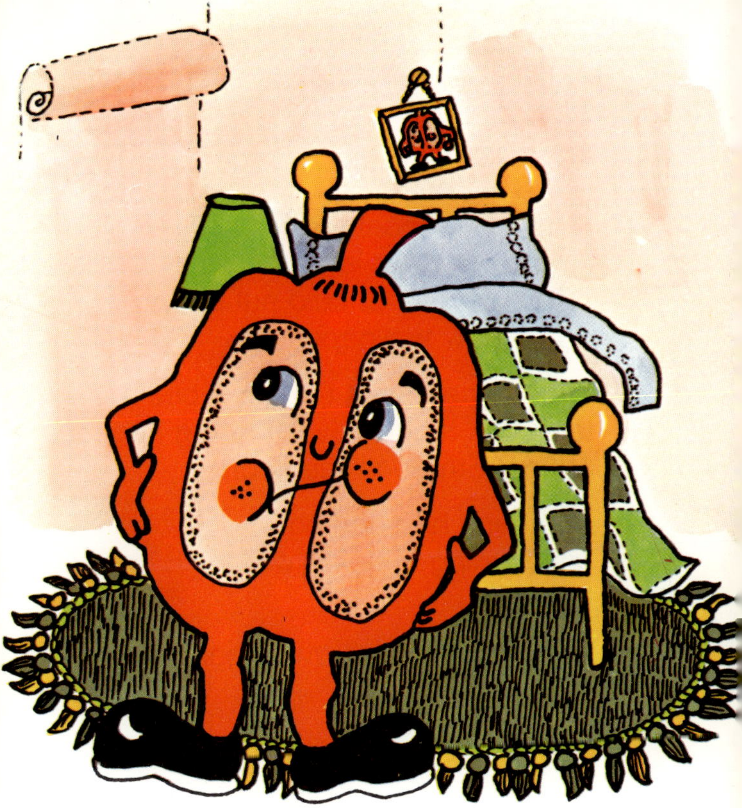

"Hm," he thought to himself, "that wallpaper is looking a little tatty. Maybe I should put up some new wallpaper."

He stepped back to take a better look, but tripped over the rug and fell right through the floor!

"Bother!" he shouted, "everything is going wrong today."

Pete Pepper was even more angry now.

Pete went into his kitchen to make himself a pot of tea.

As he poured the tea, the teapot slipped onto the table and broke into lots of little pieces.

The tea splashed all over the walls and the floor.

"Oh no! Not another disaster!" shouted Pete.

Crash! Bang! Crash!

Noises still came from Tom's house.

"I'm going to have a bath. Perhaps I can get some peace there," thought Pete angrily.

As he was running the bath there was a knock at the door.

"Hello. Is anybody home?" called a voice.

It was Tom Tomato.

"What do you want, Tom?" snapped Pete.

"I just wondered if you wanted to borrow my wallpaper and glue," said Tom cheerfully.

"No I don't," growled Pete Pepper.

As Tom walked out of the house, he slammed the door so hard that the handle fell off!

Pete Pepper was very angry now, and to make matters worse he could feel drops of water falling on his head.

"Oh no!" he cried, "I have left the bath-taps on!"

Pete Pepper rushed upstairs to see what was happening.

The bathroom was flooded.

Everything was soaked!

Poor Pete Pepper nearly burst into tears. Nothing had gone right for him today.

"I'll have to clean it all up now," he moaned.

And he started to mop up the mess.

At last Pete had finished.
He was very tired and very, very cross.

"I'm going back to bed," he said angrily. "I'm fed up."

As he sat in bed he noticed that something was different.
"The noise has stopped," he thought happily. "Now I can get some sleep."

But poor Pete could not sleep.

He tossed and turned and coughed and yawned but he still couldn't sleep.

Poor Pete. He kept thinking of all the awful things that had happened to him that day.

“It’s no good!” shouted Pete as he climbed out of bed.
“I’m going to see Tom.”

He dressed and stamped round to Tom’s house.

Tom had finished his decorating. He was drinking a cup of tea and admiring his work.

"Hello Pete," said Tom. "Why are you looking so angry?"

"It's too long a story," said Pete. "Everything has gone wrong today."

"Do you mind if I borrow your ladder and your brushes? I have decided that I will decorate after all."

After all – nothing else could go wrong today.

Or could it?

Acknowledgement: This story of Pete Pepper was adapted by Giles Reed, from an original idea by Debbie Cattermole.